STORIES FROM UNDER MY HATS

A Feminist Perspective

Poems, Prose, and Songs

Katie O'Regan

Sacred Noise Society and
The Star City Film Festival
www.sacrednoisesociety.org

This book is dedicated to my Mother Leona O'Regan. She was the wind beneath my wings as a writer and woman

CONTENTS

Sacred Noise…

"An inner noise, that is personal to all. The hidden voice that leads to the creative personal power within us all… if you listen, you can hear your Sacred Noise…" *Katie O'Regan*

"JADED IN MY JADE"

In my day, I've had the great fortune to be an ornament on many a well cuff-linked arm.
Due to my good fortune I have been kept from harm.
I have gained wisdom into the inner workings of so-ci-ety…
from Boston, to New York, to Mi-am-i…

However, this wisdom has not spared me being miserable,
I fear…I have become a rather jaded individual…
You see, I fell in love with a musician named Danny, who really broke my heart, and it knocked me on my fanny.
And after he dumped me he sent me a jade, stone, ring…that looked rather smart…
(Everyone says Ahhhhh") but it didn't take away the sting…
He told me it reminded him of my beautiful green… eyes…
He said he'd remember all the good times,
and he said who would ever get me, would be a very lucky guy…
(Chorus)
So I was alone quiet and weary, beholden to none,
I tried to be cheery, and get something done…
but I was jaded in my jade…I became… jaded in that jade…
masqueraded by his parade…wore that ring on my neck on a chain…

swore to God I'd see him again…
(Music Break)
I promised myself ten years back I'd never let him
get me…
No kissing on the first date, no chasing him away,
I tried to understand all the times he strayed…
Never begged him to come back after all the times he
went away…
Didn't know, all I was, was just a clown in his
parade…

I guess my standards were low, and my visions high.
Guess I look like one of those people who they'd just
like to try…
Naïve enough not to know that most men are just
ramblin' Joe's…
Never sold my soul, my body's been loved for free…
God knows I've had some fun… in spite of me…
(Chorus) But I was jaded in that Jade…
I became… jaded in that jade…masqueraded by his
parade…
Wore that ring on my neck on a chain… swore to
God I'd see him again…

And then one night, I went out for a night on the
town,
I donated that jade ring to some other clown…
Next day I wrote Dan a letter, though I knew he
would frown,
It said, "Dear Danny, You asshole!
My eyes are brown!"

My COLUMBUS

I've been swimming in corporate apathy
Delegated to run with the powers that be.

I've been working with so many danger zones
In the realm of backstabbing corporate homes

I've hearing what's it's like to be an independent
Source for me

I've been hopingI could make the steer
But I'm thinking I gotta' get out of here.

God knows I'm trying hard to be the
Girl for the right job

But I know who's me
And I this job and me aren't meant to be

So I'm praying to keep my check
On bank account laying

But guess what sister/ there are no guarantees
From a system that backs up there warranties

And here's how it looks…
The contract covers the feeble…
all bad hooks.

They covered my insurance
And to the retirement account,

I'm motivated to apply
But that would just keep me handcuffed to a bunch
Of Corporate lies

But I don't think sooooo…
I wish me Good luck finding my soul
In this corporate role…

They got power on there mind
They got slavery and military confines…
Even though the auspice goes

study the brain. the heart and the soul…
supposedly give us freedom for our lives…
I don't really think sooo…

"We are diplomatic, educators,
research of illuminations…
we are historical bound by donors
who need their voice out to the owners…
of businesses that care for the plight
of the weak the weak and sick

so far I know that the agenda is thick
with propositions for the grants
study the brain. the heart and the soul…
supposedly give us freedom for our lives…
I don't really think so…

(quickly said)

From the worries of our kidney's hedonistic
Drinking, pill popping probing test oriented
Better be sick, thank god the insurance will pay for…
Our perfect on site insurance payin'
the documents are right …when they're reading…

study the brain. the heart and the soul…
supposedly give us freedom for our lives…
I don't really think sooo…

God knows…we don't need it…
But we need to give them jobs
'cause we promised the kids when they were kids if
they grew up to study sides.

They would mark the world proper
With their studies with the doctors
And make a difference.

So we oblige there studies,
And we oblige the world
Proper

Beauty in a Bucket

I'm a girl who owns my wrinkles
Traveled long and hard to get 'em
and I'll have to end…
Botox ain't my friend.

whenever I look preet lill' mirror…
I wonder all about the models and their fears
I've had some one or two myself
I've questioned my colors a time or two…
And I've changed them to see what it would do

at the end day or the end of the week
at the end of the month i tell myself
it just don't matter cause fuck it
my true colors are my wealth…

just fuck it
just fuck it
bottles in a bucket
peroxide blonde brunette and red can't color me
beautiful instead,
the grey my doubt has made, bout my beauty, my
lovers my gifts and my pride
so fuck it. It's just beauty in a bucket.

GOD LOVE THE WORKIN' MAN

My heart was so secure…
so easy and true…
I had a life, a life where I was sure…
a life full of love and lure…
I was a regular working guy…
all the benefits on my side …

Had a good paycheck, and wife at home
thought I had the world by the tail…
never cheated, That's all I thought I needed to do…
Two children proper from the load
I was just a workin' guy…

One day twenty years of life;
became twenty years of pain;
the jealousy and rage,
brought a day I can't forgive…

Those papers look like monsters…
like childhood nightmare dreams…
The lawyers looked vultures
from Mack-a-million days…
…I 'm just a workin man…

Lost my children and my wife…
plenty thousands paychecks all got axed;
My dignity losts its name;
and my credit cards suddenly all were maxed.

My confidence that I grew in…

became confident I stewed in…
…and life became,,, a blurr…
(Music break)
The long cold nights, the loss of hope,
became my melody of quiet strokes…
cause I'm just a workin' man…

She'll get my pension,
and the only house I ever built
She gets my children…
And The only dream willed…
…God Love the workin' man…

GRILLING FORKS

I saw a shooting star tonight
I wished upon a dream
I called to my guardian angel to tell me what it means

They said girl of mine don't wonder why
those things you'll never really know…
They must of have known
I just left home with my bags packed for leavin'

Four kids and my husband were grillin' steaks
The perfect life I couldn't take…
A proper world with proper folks

No love from him just grillin' forks.
No fun and love and fantasy,
No quiet days when I can breathe

She said…turn around the car right now
You can make it what you want…

Your prison is filled with bliss, your
Just confused and actin like this…

It's about faith and happiness in every little moment
It's about hope and lovilness that comes across you
every day.

Just open eyes…you have prize that is worth keepin'

The kids you gave life too are only little soldiers,
Don't blame them for the things they've done…
they'll show you when they're older…

She said, "You have a heart, the will to live, and a
family watchin' out for you that
Loves you with all their might…
And that's what that shooting star meant to tell you
tonight."

UCCI LASS

Yeah… I'm a Gucci lass…
and you can kiss my Gucci ass
Wasn't born on the wrong side of the tracks
Don't apologize for my money stack

You think your better than me
Cause you're poor and lonely?

You think your think your cute
Cause you're without loot?
You think I'm proper
You think I'm prissy
You think my corporate job makes me a Goddamn
Sissy?

Oh honey are you oh so wrong
I'm just a tough bitch who refuses to be broken
You can't get me down
Cause you see I can be seen all around
Oh yeah I've been around…

Just because my grammar is proper…
And my clothes all show stoppers
And my eloquent soliloquies make your heart seem
all at ease.
Huh! I've been around… not a clown in my walk
around gown

*P*UTTIN' ALL GEARS ON HIGH

…I just did my hair dark *(Cha Cha beat)*
Put on some makeup… *(cha Cha beat)*
…I just Painted my nails…
and jumped on the scale…
(short music break "Fosse like dance moves danced)
I just sipped on some juice…
Wheat and blue-ber-ry.
I just stretched out my thighs…
Putting all gears on highhhhhhhhh!

(Chorus fast rockin' beat)

I'm turnin' myself around baby…
I'm makin' a new new me…
I'm turnin' myself around baby.
Setting that old girl free…

"THE PIE SONG"

I've only loved one man, really loved one man.
Who'd have guessed, that I would actually have a
man that I always miss…
He's the only one that I ever really miss.

All the rest were just filling in the pie…
I'd like to say I was in love with more, but I can't lie…
They were all just filling in the pie…
And hell…there's always more filling for the pie…

What's the filling without the skin?
Filling needs something to hang out in.
We had the surface! We had so much, skin…
(Quickly)
They had no crust, no whipped cream, no nutty
toppings,
No coconut sprinkles, no tarts for the popping.
All they were, were just filling in the pie…
Not like you and I…
(Music Echo)
But hopes not lost, and nor am I…
Because oh dear God…I still love pie.

(Music picks up quickly)
Pecan pie, banana cream,
Apple strudel and lemon dream,
Oreo cookie pies from Dairy Queen…

(Music Break)

Key lime… so sublime…
Peanut butter chocolate, anytime…
Popped my cherry after eating pie with a guy named
Larry…
…Who served me…an incredible slice…!

(Music Break)
I'd like to order the one that I love most
But they're out; I was told, by the host.
Hell with it! I'll just order some eggs and toast!

ⱯTEACHERS SONG

Here I am at my desk at school and I think I'm a
damn fool
Because I'm supposed to know how to teach these
kids out loud
And well today I can't remember any words
And can't seem to find any nerve
You see I need some advice and answers
to help this little girl I know who is a dancer…

Cause I am one lost little girl
Built in a body a mature woman's world
Who's a teacher right now
Trying to do the right thing somehow…
I don't know how to give to my kids
the wisdom to the heart that my teacher once did.

They look at me with beautiful eyes
They think that I hung the moon in the sky…
They ask me for my sweet guidance
and I pray to get rid of my flaws sweet riddance…

Oh give me the words, give me the words
Give me the words that I once heard…

If I had a magic a bottle that could spread all the
knowledge
I promise that I'd quit all my things and build a new
college

But since I'm a just one small teacher
Without the breadth of your great knowledge
I'm not sure I can do it
Without the help of gone scholars…

Bring me a line to tell children…
How they she they should be with their friends and
kindred

They could be could be marked
They could be hurt
They could be wrongly lead
And If that is the case, take me instead

They could be could be marked
They could be hurt
They could wrongly lead
And If that is the case take me instead

OPRAH'S MOTHER

That's right I was listening to Oprah and psychoanalysis on her show. That's right I think this is good information. Oprah gets the best. She can afford it. Thank GOD

I had an ah ha moment…like she did on her show.

She was talking to a woman and she said if you were born to a woman, your mother, who didn't love herself you model her behavior.

So if you don't love yourself and you only love those that you care for, you don't really model what a mother should model.

So I get from that… if your Mother didn't love herself but only sacrificed for you. rethink everything about what you think of yourself, because you probably don't love yourself either… and you won't pass on the wealth.

So change your mind. Cut off your idea of what you think you should be in the shadow of your Mother… because you aren't her. You are you. And just be you.

That's why Oprah is Oprah. She's just her.

HIGHER SELF EMPOWER

Higher self empowerment…
deliver me this hour –ommm

Let me meditate to ninth degree
Sacrifice my body… for thee…

Higher self empower
Deliver me this ho-u-rrrr…

Rock it now!!!! *(drums)*
Umf umf umf umf!
Rock it now!!!
Umf umf umf umf umf

Higher self empower
I'm a lady… a of the hou-ur

Hot today…
gone tomorrow…
Might as well have this one good hour.

Higher self empower…
Deliver me this hour…
Got a red bracelet, on my wrist
A strong belief, I can't resist…

Higher self empower…
Deliver me this hou-rrr…

(drums)

Umf umf umf umf!
Rock it now!!!
Umf umf umf umf umf
Rock it now.

Got a BUDDA belly
I can't explain
Got some BUDDA jelly… on my brain…

Higher self empowerment…

Deliver me this hour…

HIPS HANGOVERS AND HEADACHES

The only thing that job ever caused me was hips
hangovers and headaches
Hips, hangovers and headaches…

Slap some stuff on my plate
My last emotion I just ate
What telling me to stay at home
Cause this damn job aint nuthin but wrong

I GOT A RICH WIFE'S JOB

…I got a rich wife's job…
I hang around all day long…
I get my hair done…
… and my nails are done…
dinner is catered at five…

I have a rich wife's job
I'm a proper slob
A debutante and a slave
A regular brilliant naivete

I have a rich wife's job
I hang around all day long
My husband makes the dough
And I keep him in a roll

I have a rich wife's job.
I'm blond by peroxide
I'm rich from my bedside
I went to college to get a degree
And it turned out that I love laun-der-ry

I have rich wives friends songs,
and friends that aren't around long

I fund-raise and
Raise the kids
I worry about my
Eye-lids

I got rich wife's job
I know… that I'm privileged.
I know I could take my husband for
Every dime that he got

But I know I could be replaced for
A younger one more better
Or one just as hot

I got a rich wife's job
I hang around all day long
I go to lunch with the circuit,
But I would rather join the circus.
Cause I got a rich wife's job

A DAY FULL OF NOTHING

If today were a story and I were telling it tomorrow, I'd say I was fairly happy yesterday. I'd say yesterday was a great Saturday afternoon, a lovely rainy day…a day full of wonder because I had nothing to do but write.

That's a good day for me. A day that I have nothing to do but write. Of course I always have something to do other than write, but I just chose not to have anything to do but write. Good for me.

I could have been doing other things filling this day with lots of things that looked like what I was doing was very productive, but it really wouldn't have been that productive. Not really. Not from my point of view.
To me the mark of successful productivity is finding a day just to write and create. I call them "Days full of Nothing."

A day full of nothing promises all sorts of possibilities because it has blank space to fill.
Every minute of quiet in a day full of nothing is something full of peace, even as I work.
I hope you have many "Days of Nothing" for yourself.
Tell everyone you are terribly busy if you can darling.

THE PEACEFUL LARK

Do I speak to you in sound…?
Do I hear my heart beat… like theater in the round…?

Are my neighbors yours as well?
Or do I spot my ink in quiet wells?

The sound of you-
The quiet heart-
The humble note-
The peaceful lark…

Are my neighbors yours as well?
Or do I spot my ink in quiet wells?
In the street that goes in cycles now…
we all think we're happy now…
But do you see that same soft sound?

Now that you're here;
I see you near, I feel your face,
You are my dear, you are so near…

The sound of you-
The quiet heart-
The humble note- The peaceful lark-

The guy who shows… what is the show
The man who lives,
the highest stakes
what is that is, fades from the lake…

Show me the stage, show me the way
show me the stairs, all the way up there.

Just a beat in your heart …
A moment in time,
Fast rhythm to start,
a rhythm that's mine.
The sound of you-
The quiet heart-
The humble note-
The… peaceful… lark…

$\mathcal{L}$ET IT FLOW

A ONE, A TWO, A ONE, TWO, THREE!

Let it flowwww baby
Breathe sloooow baby
Let it goooooo baby!
Get in the flooooowww baby
5,6,7,8

Just let it floooowwwww baby
Hear your heart sloooooooow baby!

Breeaaatthhhhheeeee!!!! 5,6,7,8
Don't let it hiiiiiide baby!

You're groove's got nothin' to proooovee …Oucheeee
(smoothly)
Breaaattthhheeee
Ouch, Ouch, Ouch (They twirl)
It'll set your mind spinnin'" for a dream…

Just get in the flooooow baby
Let it goooooo baby!

Ouch!

THE GIRLS IN SAUDI ARABIA

And the girls in Saudi Arabia,
will be kickin' it and havin' some fun.
Heaven knows that's how it goes, you got to trust
someone.

Hong Kong afri-ca, the netherlands and Ireland
all around this great big world
music rules with simple tools

An ipod, a radio, bells and whistles got to blow
friendly fellows change the channels
making' mixes on their mantles

Pretty soon this globe will go
more global than you'll ever know

Europe churches young and old
playin blues and black banjos
Asian monasteries from on high
getting' down with American goods and pumpkin pie

Families from every nation
will rise from ignorance in race relations
With raps made up from coffee cups
learning math while cooking sup.

No more silence in the room
when music can have a boom

African tribes playing Mozart Alive
The Metropolitan opera with a new vibe

…and the girls in Saudi Arabia are kickin' it
and havin' fun…

Do I NEED SOMEBODY

Every once in my family will say.
How's your love life darling? Is it still the same?
Don't you need somebody
Don't you need someone?
Maybe should go on a date
before it's way too late…
(*blues*)
And I always back like this.
In a historical, metaphorical, rhetorical way…

Do I need somebody
Do I need someone
I think that could be fun…

Do I need somebody
Do I need someone

Do I need somebody
If I did that would I be done?
Or would I want to run?

You see,
I've always been in love with the very same man
He's very independent
and slightly redundant
He likes traveling and singleness and traveling and freedom
and freedom and singleness and traveling
and freedom and occass-ion-aly
he likes me to be…in a place where he sometimes can
always see me.

Do I need somebody
Do I need someone?

Maybe he would really keep my heart
like he has for all these years?
and plant my feet upon the ground
and take away my tears?

I think it could work permanently
I've always thought it so
I got up the nerve to say it about a year ago,
and he told me no...
(*Key change*)

...and he said we can still be friends and meet up
every now and then again
after all these years we both need somebody,
We both need someone.

It sure 's been knowing you
Have a fun with your freedom
and your traveling to
...and on my way out
I left him with this thought...

Yes I need somebody
Yes I need some fun
Yes I need somebody
...let's get it done!

Yes I say yes to love
Yes I say yes me
Yes I say yes to lovin'
what a lovely place to be!

A PRAYER FOR LIGHT

Light to the world Light to our hearts

Light to all of our dark parts

We pray for humor

We pray for peace

We pray for the hungry and to let bombs cease

We pray to make hatred to go away

We pray for some time to let our hearts play

We pray for a moment of beauty and security we pray
our nerves tension to melt into

obscurity Whether we pray and say "OMMMM" or
if whether we pray and say "Glory Be"

Let's pray for our differences to sink to the sea.

THIRTY MINUTES

Today I shall waste some time. My mind wanders, my soul ponders… I can't think of a solitary useful thing to do with my day Therefore, I wish to give this time away! Today I will deposit my 24 hours in a time machine for other's good use. To be productive is a must! …So, to balance my days wanderlust… …I will become a philanthropist! I will open an account at the nearest financial center, and in the bank's investment ledger my name will be entered… …under an account, called "Smell the Roses" With my account set up, on the very first day. and I'd divvied it up this very way… …30 minutes too a lucky person just too keep-em on a role… 30 minutes for a tired Mom to keep so she'd have 30 minutes to sleep… 30 minutes to a random neighbor, so they could have a shot at an extra 30 minute bonus time slot… 30 minutes to a person who cleans the streets at night… 30 minutes to a new business owner, so they could take a breath… 30 minutes to a steel worker, so they could have a rest. 30 minutes to a School Teacher, so they could eat their apple. 30 minutes to the bank teller in the bank so she has a long lunch … to put her in a good disposition for the 5:00 customer time crunch. 30 minutes to a postman just because they never get a break. 30 minutes to a lottery winner, so they could enjoy their feast. 30 minutes to 12 children, who have inventions they want to create… 30 minutes to a Grandma so she could dance away her cares. 30 minutes to a Grandpa so he could comb his wife's white hair. And that would make my Smell the Roses bank account kaput! For the very first day, my 24 hours of good time is used all the way.

Angel in the Light Bulb

A light bulb flashed and flickered near my entrance door to my little apartment in New

York City. I went to see which bulb in the crystal light fixture went out. I was

disappointed and surprised because first of all it's difficult to change those bulbs because

The light fixture is so heavy and the ceiling is high. Second of all, I normally don't have to

change those bulbs often, and I had just changed them one week prior. Third of all it

reminds me that I have to dust…again! As I walked over to look at the light in the ceiling,

I noticed that the entrance door was not closed all the way though I thought I had closed

it and locked it of course. I was thankful that that bulb went out because I would have

never checked the door before I went to sleep, and I do live in New York City! I silently

said a quick thank you prayer and this thought went across my mind, "I must have an

angel here with me tonight!" Very quickly I heard
something so beautiful that chills ran
up my arms. It was the sound of a loud flutter of
wings right over my head filling the

sound waves of my apartment. And if it weren't so
absolutely silly to think that angels

could actually come visit people, I would swear there
was an angel in that lightbulb.

TONGUE IN CHEEK FOR ASTROLOGY FREAKS

We are Luna…tick.tick.tick.ticktiiiiiiccks We are sick sick sick sick sick …We watch the moon …We watch sky …We watch the clock of time go by We are Luna tick tick tick tick tickssss We plan out days We plan our nights by the ticking of the skies. We are astrologically challenged, addicted to the stars Our lives are controlled by Jupiter, Venus and Mars We are lunatic tick tick tick ticks We are sick sick sick sick sick. The farmer's almanac and Egypt started it all. The pyramids sundial, The ancient scrolls, Decided our fate years ago. We are destined to be crazy. It says so in our charts: We dream of aroraboroleus, asteroids and rising signs all night! We are luna tick tick tick tick ticks We are sick sick sick sick sick Your sun sign says you're practical, Your rising says you're hot Your moon says you're serious But your boyfriend says you're not. All these things make us crazy. So maybe it was better in the old age But really nothing has changed, Except now they call them psychics not sage. The groundhog predicted six more weeks And Neptune defunct his claim, The planet of Mars has gone retrograde And the stocks in the market have done the same Some politicians are all full of shit. It's mid February… and that's it …and the protesters are far into March. We are luna tick tick tick tick ticks!

$\mathcal{A}$ LOVE POEM

Love informs art…It inspires genius…makes poets out of fools…crosses rivers without notice…fights battles without swords,and relishes dilemma in the name of it's face. Loves calms disease…gives hope to the needy and serves none but itself. Love is…large and strange and plentiful plainness. Love is both rhyme and verse…full of color and tasteless. Nothing to see and elusive to touch.'Till time is love, there is no boundaries to it.'Till one can chew love, there is no recipe to it. As a witness to itself, it seeps in the darkest of places and consumes its counterpart.

Apparent as an apple, as applicable as it's seed…Love begins and ends and ends to begin.

I THINK IT HAPPENED IN THE YEAR 2003

There was a time when all the world thought that living was for attaining, competing, winning, getting' over, being the best, having the most toys, the finest taste defined by neighborhood and labels, and now we live in a different time. Though there are hanger-oners, to that thought. They have become not cool in the collective conscience. The cutting edge of cool now is the cool that can't be judged by the book's cover. The heart of our memorable existence lies in the heart of a person's character, our knowledge, our allotment for love, our joy, our unspeakable passions, our wit and our ability to inspire. On the journey as humans in our time in life, we are all asked to embrace this beautiful "New Hipness". Though we still love beauty, we always will, this is not the biggest problem…for beauty is good. Our biggest problem, or challenge rather, is to recognize beauty, the type that changes people…the type that inspires…the type that means something in regard to how it helps, heals, gives and inspires. Because indeed our greatest worth is to help our greatest weakness. Indeed our greatest weakness is those that don't see and don't have the means to do so. So in this New Year, I call upon myself, and my muse to help inspire those that can't see, and to listen to those that do so that I can be of bigger service. All that we have in this short life is the talents that we were given and the fortitude that allows us to serve no matter what our professions are.

I wish you all love, happiness, great inspiration and
true beauty in this year…
I think it happened in the year 2003.

My RED BIKE

I tap the tallest tree and ask it what it sees way up there. As I ride my old red bike that reads "Free Spirit" on it's faded cross bar, I marvel at the flowers still in bloom, still in bloom. I fall to the ground and kiss the dirt to feel the earth I walk on. But don't get me wrong. I'm not that reverent. The fall wasn't on purpose. I take off my hat in the coldest wind and listen for what it has to say. I silently close my eyes in the dark, as I wish my fears away. But I don't wander along in the wind too long… I don't talk to the tree so long that I wonder about myself. I don't kiss the ground so long that it becomes dirt instead of earth. You see, I fit my poems between my days, so that I can live in the world, but still walk on the earth as a citizen of the planet. Those quiet trees have a way of keeping my feet planted, but letting my mind fall like red leaves twirling slowly to the ground. Soft landings are imminent. Human nature is both good and evil I suppose. We as humans are a part of nature. I hope I can stay on nature's good side for as long as I live. It's much more pleasant that way. If it so happens that the breeze of nature's evil side catches me while I was amazed by the flowers, someone please remind me about those silver linings, and point me to the direction of my red bike "Free Spirit".

November 22, 1963

Here's to the one I'd take a bullet for …the beautiful wild creative working woman, who gave birth to her creatures like a deer in the night who comforted to those with unwilling hearts, who calmed the darkest fears, who made light of tragedies nobody could bare, who's faithful servitude made people out of animals, and scholars out of pancakes, who's humble quietness made dignified men, and gave hope to one little girl that maybe she could do the same. Here's to the one I'd take a bullet for, for without her, I could see no light in my lot as a woman. A model of femininity, she gave presence to me. I hold strongly in my heart, that all women have a chance to do just the same. In the fall of her life, the beauty that she radiates, accomplishes the glow, that she held tightly as a dream, as a girl. Here's to the one I'd take a bullet for… I was in her womb when that quiet large day, when Kennedy in his Texas convertible met his fate, with flowers strewn and his wife in tow. It is as though it was yesterday, in that quiet floating place, when I heard her say, "Don't worry honey. It's going to be okay."My bullet will be when she dies. …But then I will see her in heaven, when God will grant his shining crown on her, and for my grace, me as well. We will both giggle at the day when I was in her womb and she was a scared girl. She'll say to me, "Remember when I said, "Don't worry honey. It's going to be okay?" and I'll say, "Yes Mama, I remember." …and she will say, "See I told you so!"

My bullet will be when she dies. ...But then I will see her in heaven, when God will grant his shining crown on her, and for my grace, me as well. We will both giggle at the day when I was in her womb and she was a scared girl. She'll say to me, "Remember when I said, "Don't worry honey. It's going to be okay?" and I'll say, "Yes Mama, I remember." ...and she will say, "See I told you so!"

On Gratitude

Gratitude for the gift of freedom, creativity, awareness and wonder.

Gratitude for the many moments of unexpected joy that those days bring.

Gratitude for the times I am not lonely though I am often alone.

Gratitude for my fingers that can type, my will that is determined,

…my heart that is strong, my legs that carry me where I choose to go.

Gratitude for the books that people have written that I absorb in a beautiful private world they've created.

I feel

Gratitude for the three ladies down the street in the small corner store who get up every morning, go to work and make that wonderful steaming coffee and those fresh biscuits that I love enjoy when I'm traveling in my car to this place or that place.

I feel

gratitude for the people whom I teach in classes, because without them, I wouldn't have people in my classes to be grateful for.

I feel

gratitude for anyone who teaches me anything, because without them I wouldn't know too much.

Mostly I feel… gratitude for anyone who reads this, because that means you care. Thanks for that.

FINDING WHAT WE HAVE…

We may get jealous of the things that other people have. Maybe we can feel bad for what we haven't accomplished in our life compared to others. But the funny thing is, is that we really are all the same, we just wear different hats at different times in our lives. The key is to enjoy the ride, when the ride has the wheels to be available. Even when we are famous, Even when we are the best, Even when we are the richest person in the world… Or when are the most gifted leader, the most talented dancer, singer, or actor in history of our chosen genre… we still only may love one person for real at one time, we still are only one parent, no matter the number of children, we still may be only one Godmother, Godfather or Grandparent to one two special children… or maybe one uncle or aunt who makes the difference. If we have no family, maybe the people that we work with everyday are our real family. These things, these people, are who make us whole and happy and at the end of the day. These things are the things that define our hearts and our characters at different times in our lives. The interesting thing that we all experience, is that none of us get it all at once. What we do get is the opportunity to watch and appreciate others who are enjoying the different "rides' ' of life, that we are not. This can be as beautiful as experiencing it ourselves. That's why we don't ever have to be jealous or sad for what we are lacking. We wouldn't have the opportunity to appreciate all the gifts if we got them all at the same time. We can do many things in life. We just can't do it all at once. There is always the opportunity to do what we are meant to do, if we believe that is what we need. It's in the appreciation for what we do have, in where we are blessed. It all comes in increments,this beautiful thing we call love.

Home Song

I've left a lot a lot chances, I've let some good dreams go… to get to the place, that makes me whole… I've traveled some distance, and taken the long way around… Stepped over some manholes, and stared up to heaven… to find my way home, to my safe haven. Now I've got a log fire burning, and I've got a hot stove cooking… I've got a warm bedded bed, and I'm not leaving, this safe haven, for nothing… My safe haven is the place I've made… It took a lot of work; it took a lot of pay, just to make it here… it's the way I wanted it to be… When you're a guest, of the place I grew, We'll write stories that we weave, We'll laugh as much as we breathe… My safe haven is yours too… We all need a place… that we've made home… No matter what the price, no matter where we've roamed… through the arms of our safe haven may be tight, they feel free… My safe haven is a place I've made… it took a lot of work; it took a lot of pay, just to make it here… the way I wanted it to be… Flowers smell sweeter when you've planted the seeds… The sweeter is the warmest when you've tied the knots. The memories are the sweetest, at a long journey's end… My…safe…haven…

Quiet Julie

One afternoon in her school hallway, Julie sat in a corner ready to leave.
Her coat was on her back and she had already quit.
She couldn't take another day
of it.
She left the school without telling a soul.
She'd packed her music books under her bed at home.
She was only sixteen… When Julie was ten, she was the serious kind she
I loved music and she was blind to all the things that were wrong in the world.
I was her teacher and she was my girl, she would tell me after class that I was her world… That April I asked Julie what was wrong one day. She said she'd lost her dad and her Mom ran away, and now they had to move her again… They told her… Try not to talk too loud. Try not to be too proud. Don't sing so strongly. Don't talk too loud, don't sing so strong. Don't
Tell me your feelings in your heart, There's no hope for being who you are. Don't be so proud…And don't talk too loud… Talk of hiding and not of seeing and remember the following: Don't talk too loud … don't sing too proud. Go to someplace where you are far away, it'll be safe there… Like a child who's not heard, Like a broom that can't sweep, Like an apron around tiny bound feet She couldn't stay there… Julie whispered her hopes so that they wouldn't stare … She didn't say it out loud, but she said, I'm outta'

here… They said… Couldn't you lose some weight, couldn't you trim your hair, don't you know pretty girls are treated more fair.

 They said, "Quiet that song that sings in your heart. Cover your wounds so that they won't talk, and don't talk too loud… Don't talk too loud Don't talk too loud Don't sing

so strong… Like a child who's not heard Like a broom that can't sweep

like an apron around her tiny bound feet. She couldn't stay there… Don't talk too loud… Don't talk too loud…

 Don't sing so strong

Julie was found in L.A., alone in the dark. She'd lost all her weight and her hair was short. The needle that gave her the courage to sing, took the life out her and the breath out of me. With her music books

still packed under her bed at home, I couldn't help but think why I couldn't have helped more. You see I was the one that taught her to dance. She took

my voice class the year after that. Last summer she was my student at the theater in the park, and this year they all decided she was getting too proud, … and that's all she heard… I say… Talk too LOUD… SING too LOUD. Sing so strongly… I say… Talk too LOUD… SING too LOUD… Sing so strongly…

I say… Talk too LOUD… SING too LOUD… Sing so strongly…

THE CORPORATE RIVER

When I saw CORPORATE America and dreamed to be in its midst, I saw a Massive RIVER of Wealth, Power, Promise, Depth, and Progress. I saw a STRUCTURE that Flowed and gave birth to new lives within its organism. I saw a river that changed the LANDSCAPE of the COUNTRY it was within. So I jumped in the river in a corporate wetsuit. On the Surface of the River, I found a river that raged, with people that were more men than not. On the surface, we were all doing identical beautiful breathe-strokes, racing to win. We had waterproof starched shirts. Our wetsuits were blue, and they matched most of the racer's eyes. The blue-eyed racers of the male persuasion got loud cheers from the shores. The female versions were chased by many of the first string strokers. Beneath the surface of the River I found jungles. The jungles were thick with debris and dangerous angles. There wasn't time to explore the jungle for its beauty. We had breathe-strokes to do. One day I saw the sun shine so bright on the ripples ahead of me, I stopped stroking, went against the current and swam to the bank. I was concerned for many of my fellow breathe-strokers as I swam away.

$\mathcal{D}$IME STORY PHILOSOPHY

I love the idea of a Dime Store. Where I grew up in Northeast Iowa, there was one particularly wonderful Dime Store in our neighboring town of New Hampton. This town was about a half hour away from the farm that my six brothers, my parents and I grew up on. The Dime Store was called The Ben Franklin Dime Store. That store holds vivid memories of Christmas shopping for new toys starting in August, squirt guns, silly puddy, jawbreakers, plastic fairy princess jewelry sets, marshmallows, Barbie dolls, sleds, precious jeweled rings, fancy earrings, $5 tennis shoes, BIG Candy bars, and my Mother's ideas about what was good, or not. Though, my Mother isn't an overly opinionated woman, I have many memories of my Mother's opinion connected to the Ben Franklin Dime Store. Thankfully they are all quite pleasant memories. My favorite trips to New Hampton were when just Mom and I would go. Perhaps it fulfilled our need to escape the overriding masculinity of the O'Regan household. At times we would quickly plan our trips, assured that the boys probably "didn't have time to come with us" and we would be off in our station wagon to New Hampton. It's not that Mom didn't adore her sons, because she most certainly did. It's not that I didn't think my brothers were cool to be around and fun, because they were. We just needed to be girls. Mother loved to browse and say hello to the clerks and be pleasant to people. She always had a way with strangers that way. She still does only maybe even more so with age. Mom has this calming effect on strangers. She would usually crack a lady-like joke to one of the familiar check out girls that would make me laugh too. We would often run into one of the church ladies from our hometown Parish who would be in New Hampton shopping as well. They would always be so happy to see Mom and would usually make a comment about how I was growing up, and isn't it wonderful that my Mother had at least one daughter. I guess that always made me feel special, though I didn't realize it at the time. When we went to New Hampton, we would often go to garage sales to pick up a treasure or two, or go to the fabric store to find some good cloth to make a nice dress or top out of. Of course I always wanted new clothes, but even as a child, I appreciated that my Mother knew how to spin gold out of straw. Indeed she did with her remakes of old clothes turning them into original creations. She even took the time to teach me how to do it. After checking out the sites on the "yet to be hip vintage clothes scene", Mom and I would go to the Ben Franklin Dime Store for essentials. After a visit with Mr. Franklin we would go Grocery shopping. None of these stops always happened in order on every trip to New Hampton, but of course the grocery shopping was always the last stop because of the frozen food factor. At the grocery store we would get the super sized grocery shopping cart and coupons in hand. We would search for the weekly specials and the oversized staples that were needed to accommodate our bevy of boys at home. As I got older into High School, I would notice how friendly the check out boys were to my Mother and I. This was very curious to me, because the boys in my High School were never this overly-friendly to me. Perhaps that had something to do with the fact that I had six brothers surrounding me and all the boys at my High School knew that and the checkout boys at the store went to a different High School than my brothers and I. I don't know…just a guess… After our shopping trip we would drive slowly home, bags and bags of groceries in tow. Mom would tell me what was on her mind, and I would tell her what was on mine, and at the end of the afternoon, and a visit to old Ben Franklin's Dime store, I somehow would always feel listened to and inspired. I think Mr. Franklin and Mom have a lot in common.

LOVE AND TREASON FOR GOOD REASON

See how you always go love, See how you hold tight my heart, See how you always go love You advise my heart and break all the rules, our love is a secret, we're definitely fools. The water is, as you and I, go as it does…but the tide is faithful. See how you always go love, See how you hold my heart tight. See how you always go love… Our swept away nights, our laughter in flight, oh the far away places we fly… If you ask public opinion, our romance is a scandal, but ask the romantics who know love… They'll tell you that they have had these days in their hearts, so in love they judge no person. There are many reasons we fall to love and, to treason, all those reasons, we can't possibly know. I know today I'm not wise at all, for I'm blinded by love… and if love is truly blind, then I truly love Braille! See how you always go love See how you hold my heart tight See how you always go love.

Albuquerque

I'm moving out to albuquerque…
by a business that's perfect turnkey
A carwash with some storage units
DDA 10 room hotel
Winters I'll ski in Munch.

Drive to Sedona, weekends
Eat donuts on Tuesday and
Wednesday will be a totally new day
Thursday I'll ride big black horses
Friday I'll study Indian coursework

Sing my songs, create my diddies
Write about things far from the city
In my own land…my own land,.
Albuquerque you are grand…

A COLOR IS JUST A COLOR. ASS HOLE.

Sometimes I dye my hair to be a different color than what it naturally is… I'm a natural redhead brunette born of the Irish cloth…the red comes through. However. I have been known to be a raven brunette and a strawberry blonde. Being born Catholic, I was taught that dying your hair somehow made you a woman "who died her hair" so I never dyed my hair until I was almost 27 years old. I was afraid that people would think I was a "Woman who dyed her hair" if you know what I mean. The reason I bring this up is that today I was looking outside my front door in Sheboygan, gazing at the glorious tree that flanks my property on Superior Avenue. I noticed that it was a glorious shade of burnt red orange and I was inspired with the thought that goes something like this. Sometimes… we just want to change our shades to go along with nature. Sometimes…we want to be burnt orange, sometimes we want to be black and charcoal as a statement and sometimes we want to be green, like growing and green…like starting new and green.

So here's to our moods and the pull of the moon that makes us naturally be different shades. God bless the hairdressers that accommodate nature, as unnatural as it is. They provide a service to the ever-changing moods of the girls following the flow of the moon and the tide and the season. Life is short…so here is to the colors that we can be! A color is just a color…

I'm dying my hair bright Pink someday for sure, or
maybe just get a wig,
Men: "She's a blonde, a brunette, a redhead"
Women: "It's just A color is just a color assholes."

A WHITE CHURCH CAMP

Emma had four sisters and two best friends
A bible in her chapel hand
She was 6 years old
Holding Grandma's hand
in her Buckle shoes

Six years later, like a willow branch
She walked from her Grandma's ranch
In her Flower sundress
so she could sing
Emma's finding her wings …

Emma turns fourteen and she's baptized
The church lawn shines in her Grandma eyes

A white church camp
A yellow rose
A girl in love
Only Jesus knows
It's a white church camp
In two short years Emma learned to drive
Jimmy found a fast place in her life
Swept her away one full moon
At her white church camp
the sun rose and found her home
on the her blue bench
and old Oak tree
She looked to see if she could see
the church door still opened

She was hoping…
A white church camp
A yellow rose
A girl in love
Only Jimmy knows
It's not a white church camp
At seventeen…
Six years pass
Jimmy was the last
To know Emma came back to town
with her little girl…
in her buckle shoes…
A white church camp

A yellow rose

A girl in love

Only Jimmy knows

It's not a white church camp…At seventeen…At
seventeen

A STARBUCKS THANKSGIVING

I sit by myself with my laptop and my tall venti coffee, a whole grain biscuit slightly dry, and several lonely people watch me type. I'm in Starbucks on the north shore of Milwaukee.
Starbucks was the only place open around today. It's now 2:32 Only eight more hours of Thanksgiving to go.
I'm having a good time. I meet the staff at starbucks, talk to some strangers who see me by myself and I'm sure wonder why.
I tell them my family is far away, which is true. Well they are about 4hours away. I say I'm meeting friends later, but the truth is, I was invited to see friends but I'm going to visit them. They live 2. 5 hours away, and I'm going.
Despite this lonely picture, I'm not sad because I'm free. I'm healthy and free and I can type.
I'm thankful to Starbucks for being open too.
I decided to pull together this book called tempting fate that I have been writing for a while. It's a book of bits and pieces and small stories in my jagged life of non commitment and joy. You will see a story a day, that has nothing to do with the day that the story is attached too. This book is a celebration of everyday life being attached to nothing but the mysteries of life and my personal freedom. I call it tempting fate.

If there is someone with a heart that wants more…
I understand you.

If there is a child that something and I'm around. I'm
your gal.
If there is a daughter that has a heart to forgive, I'm
your kid.
If there is a sister that needs your shoulder, that is me.
if there is a heart that is ready for love…open to
God's calling, I stand counted…

Call me if you need encouragement, and I will
comfort you with words if I am free.

That being said, I'm no hero. You see…I have had a
fate so far that has been very temporary. Temporary
jobs, temporary friends, temporary living spaces,
temporary dreams. I have tempted fate many a day.
As I write on this dayThanksgiving Day I give thanks
for the opportunity to live such a life.
I chose my life. I chose to be alone today. I had
invitations.
I keep choosing this,
someday maybe I will choose that.
I moved to New York City without a job…twice.
Once by myself, once with a temporary boyfriend.
I call myself independent,
I am really just a fuckin' hippy at heart in heels
sometimes.
I have a fate that is meant to be temporarily available
to many and
It is true that I am a dreamer and a stranger. But I can
only have certain things expected of me I'm afraid. If
I say I'm going to do something I will do it. However,
I make promises with great caution.

I love children, but I've none of my own. I love
being a partner in a relationship, yet I cease to be in
that relationship the minute I feel as if I am being

controlled. I don't think I'm broken. You might disagree. I just think I'm independent and like to be free. Besides, that sounds much better than broken.

I am a lone wolf. A social animal, a contemplative seer, a powerful business woman, a rockin' party chick, a singer and a temporary citizen of this planet with legal papers.

I've never had a job that was stable and secure because well, why would anyone hire someone for a stable and secure job when they know that person isn't necessarily either of those two; at least not according to my resume.

"No matter where you go there you are"
2) "Take No Prisoners" are my two favorite sayings. My theory: It's better to be by yourself than to be with any type of a person who treats you badly.

May the wind of all you ancestry bless you, keep you and let you go so you can free.

FEBRUARY 6 AT MY HOUSE IN THE SNOW

I sit writing in the kitchen of the second floor of my house. The sound of a snow blower blowing hums in my ear,
reminding me of the ever changing seasons and flow of water in the air, and the plants hidden among the blanket of snow.

I find it quite beautiful; this quiet.

I unpack years of memorabilia from shows that I have created from nothing but the Spirit I had to do it.

I hang pictures from the shows on my hallway stairs walls that I pass as I walk up to my homey little apartment in the sky.

I cook simple healthy but yummy food that makes me feel good about my body.

I occasionally tinker on my friendly old baby grand that never disappoints me with it's rich surprise of tenor and tune.

I open the cover of a new book nightly, where I read until the wee hours.
This; all to nourish a tired but grateful soul.

I'm healing the past years bumps and bruises. New York City, Chicago…

They are healing rather nicely.

All this introspection beats the hell out of checking
myself into some crazy ass
recovery place or sitting in some cold cold chair
telling someone my problems of ago.

I already know what problems I have. There is no
need to repeat.

There is only need to love to forgive to gather the
good and leave the bad in the dust;
to see the light in all and to see the light that emerges
when the bumps and bruises have long gone.

That's what I've been doing.

So I GOT MY REAL ESTATE LICENSE

So I got my Wisconsin real estate license course finished. I have a New York Broker's License. I loved doing REAL ESTATE in Manhattan. But now I have moved back to Wisiconsin for a while. SO… I did it online. I was like, hell, I may as well do something productive while I'm a little lost on my journey.

You see I like to accomplish things…but then once I accomplish it I'm not all that interested. This is why being a theater producer and director are good for me.

You pick the show, plan it, get the cast and crew together, rehearse them, perform it for the public and it's done. Next! That's all.

Real Estate is like the same thing. Temporary relationships…make something move on…1. Step 1: make people smile. 2. Step 2: help someone 3. Step calm them down and make them comfortable, so they can fuckin' thing straight. Step 4. Guide them in the right direction. Step 5. Don't hate them, if they want to do something else. Step 6. I'm done already with the Wisconsin real estate thing. I won't stay here that long. Who am am I kidding.
Everything is like Real Estate.

*W*HAT IF?

So I am sitting in my boyfriend Jim and I's apartment in Milwaukee. There is a beautiful view of lake Michigan. Sale boats are out, though there are few today. It's so damn cold and It's June 15th already. Crazy weather this year.

It's quiet. Jim is gone on a Saturday visit to his old friend Jeffs leaving me alone to attend to my producing work on my musical "The Dream Café!". We are opening it seven weeks from now at the Athenaeum theater in Chicago.
It's very exciting. I have never performed in Chicago. In NEw York CIty in Miami…so many other places…it's been fun.
I'm very excited!
I'm also scared as hell. What if we fail? What if nobody buys tickets? What if the audience doesn't like my show that I worked on forever?
What if I suck on stage?
What if someone thinks I should have cast other people?
What if my cast members are mean to me? What if… oh fuck the what if's.
I'm doing it anyway!
Some things you should never know or you would never do them.

ON BEING HUMAN AND BEING CREATIVE…

As humans: no matter our titles, our wallet size, our height, our learning capabilities, our place of birth, our ancestors, we are only inches away from each other in exact similarity.

As Humans: we are only molecules in difference… nearly identical if we compare ourselves to anything else alive on this planet.

As humans: whether we are terribly fascinated with football or quantum physics…video fames or dancing, how far do our interests really differ?

At any point in time the beauty of our differences can manifest into compliment, catharsis or war.

Isn't it beautiful to have the gift of being human?

Free will and free economy create massive competition. If we live in a society where there is no free economy and free will to a large degree, humans are still in massive competition with each other, even emotionally. Competition is not a bad thing. It sustains us if our egos are detached enough from the process. Competition teaches us, and sustains us.

As humans: we are walking contradictions being born from the need to learn. While we are alive our learning can be the most painful part of our lives and the biggest joy, but usually learning comes with struggle of some sort no matter how exhilarating our learning experiences can be.

We form communities to find safety in learning, and yet our communities often become our biggest enemy. We form relationships with each other to have walls to bounce our ideas off of and to admire the creation of energy that happens when individual's worlds collide. We do this if not consciously but sub-consciously.

We are constantly creating thoughts by words, by action, by smiles and by the slightest choices we make.

The next time you hear someone say they are not creative, stop and imagine why they are saying that. Usually there is a deep-seated lack of confidence that is coming from.

Perhaps we just don't understand what being creative means as a society. We are creations living in the process of constant creation. Creating equals being alive. Breathing, walking, and thinking are all creative endeavors. Since we have the capability to create, we have the capability to be infinitely creative.

$\mathcal{I}$ AIN'T NO TEST DRIVE

Here's for all the girls… who've been loved by many
men…
follow me into the dream of better lovin' dreams…
Let's say it loud… let's say it proud…

I ain't no test drive…
You can't try me on for size.

This is no dealer's special for free…
I ride drivin' or riding,
but there ain't no room for three.

I'm not bettin' on you, unless you bet on me first…
'cause I ain't no test drive.

Come clean and clear with your passenger seat free,
…and I'll believe that you have room for me.
…'cause I ain't no test drive.

I've seen lots of dealers try to sell me a lease,
but I'm not lookin' for short term,
I'm lookin' to buy a car that makes me feel pleased.

I'm not interested in a quick sale…
from a fast talker's eyes,
'cause a shiny paint job is easy to find.
Under the hood, I want an engine that's mine.

I ain't no test drive

You can't try me on for size
I'm not interested in short term,
I'm lookin' to buy.

My car can drive me far and long with safety in mind,
Run me fast and far with the rotors entwined,
Shift me steady and sure with no direction for sure…
Bet on the brakes, and let the accelerator purr.

But I ain't no test drive
You can't try me on for size
I'm not interested in short term,
I'm lookin' to buy…

Here's for all the girls sing it loud. I ain't no test drive

THE BANQUET YEARS

(An Ode to the Turn of the Century while living in Manhattan)

Hello, my name is "Fen de Cecile"!
That means turn of the century
in French you see. I'm the muse of the time.
Hidden from sight all the time.
Yet my voice could be heard when they closed their
eyes.
It still can be heard if you close your eyes.
and now for a small time we've come to repeat history
awake!
We'll speak of a story hidden from ears of the years.
This story
is called "Heaven come 11" 11 years at the turn of
the century
from the eyes of the collective muse of the time.
My face is but one face of a million souls, and it is
part of
your face too.
"They were the elegant years,
lucky as elephant ears."
Some came from foreign lands
to paint all Paris grand
Edison lit stage for us clear
and I, "Fen de Ceicle" was the muse to your ears
Cezzane, Van Gough,and Picasso, Manet and Monet
Degas,

the years plucked the face of Art's eyebrows proper
and clear
They were the elegant years
we knew they'd go down in history
They knew what they knew then was currently a
mystery
Their friends all around were anxious and boding
afraid that our discoveries were frivolous, not worth
noting
They created new dance and cinema, impressions of
new the
woman…huh!
The Moulin Rouge kicked the butts of bureaucrats
and higher ups

ISADORA, SARAH, LOUIE,AND MADAME
CURIE WERE BRILLIANT MOVERS AND
SHAKERS AND NO LESS
AND THE REST WERE MEN BUT THAT'S
OKAY CAUSE HISTORY HAS GIVEN
THEM The MOST OF THE PRESS!
and now it's something like 100 years later at the turn
of the
century, "Fen De Cecile" if you may, and we're back.
These are the new elegant years, and they'll go down
in history
with glee we'll see… won't we!

A BOTTLE OF BROKEN DREAMS

It was February 2nd. I was cleaning my bathroom toilet closet filled with bottles of beautiful, but slightly forgotten small treasures. There were creams, bubbles to smooth the bath, shampoos of all types and conditioners designed to make my mane more marvelous…which is just an elegant way of saying a bunch of old useless shit.

I spotted a bottle of perfume bought in New York at the hip and fashionable store downstairs from my apartment on Broadway. It was purple and was called "dream." It's made by gap. I purchased it because I loved the smell, and because I write about dreams. Dreams are one of my major life long themes. I am a dreamer. I always have been. I have seen things in my dreams the night before they happened the next day. I have dreamed of beautiful faces I've never seen, only to meet the person that matched that face in the middle of a day.

I forgot I had this almost full bottle of fragrance called "DREAM." I was pleasantly surprised I'd forgotten it about. I picked it up and for some reason I brought it to my kitchen where my computer is. I sat it on my kitchen counter and no sooner than I did, it fell to the floor smashing in bits and pieces the sweet fragrance tarnished with glass on the floor.

My eyes welled up with tears so heavy it felt like they had just broken on the floor.

I laid my head on the kitchen table and cried. There it was, a bottle of broken dreams laying on the floor in plain sight for me to see. The jagged edge of the bottle standing on it's base upright with the word "dream" underneath it.

All the disappointment and struggle that I had experienced the last few years had walloped me in the face that day, changing my direction in life forever.

I decided to dry up and go on, just like the perfume on the floor.

Love and Treason for All Good Reasons

See how you always go love,
See how you hold tight my heart, See how you always go love
You advise my heart and break all the rules, our love is a secret, we're definitely fools.
The water is, as you and I, go as it does…but the tide is faithful. See how you always go love, See how you hold my heart tight. See how you always go love…
Our swept away nights, our laughter in flight, oh the far away places we fly… If you ask public opinion, our romance is a scandal, but ask the romantics who know love… They'll tell you that they have had these days in their hearts, so in love they judge no person. There are many reasons we fall to love and, to treason, all those reasons, we can't possibly know. I know today I'm not wise at all, for I'm blinded by love… and if love is truly blind, then I believe in Braille! See how you always go love See how you hold my heart tight
 See how you always go love.

AMERICAN QUEEN

My only you

My Mother you.

I still see you

My Mother you…

Your eyes… your eyes…

Gray hair …

My memory of you…

____

That smile

That heart

So harsh

No care

hands of steel

feet of gold

One lost to pain…

My lady dear

Miss American Queen

Lost to your dreams

cold as ice
smile so nice

Hold on my dear

Hold me near

My American Queen

You'll be alright

He'll be right there…

And so will I…

It's August 18, 2023. I have had quite the journey in the last 5.5 years. I lost both of my parents, and moved 5 gazillion times in the pursuit of doing the right thing for them. I produced a big feature film, five film festivals, published a book and bought and sold houses. I forgive myself for having my hair not perfect sometimes, for having one too many glasses of wine, when I was previously not drinking, for gaining a few pounds, when I pride myself on my flat tummy, for considering moving to Bora Bora, for dropping too many cuss words and for being too hard on the world, when everyone else is going through traumatic situations as well. I just thought I would check in with my truth my friends. I love you❤ Katie

TWOSDAY

It's 2/22/2022 today and it's Tuesday.

What can we say. Today I talked to only two people on the phone. My Father and my bff Tricia.

I didn't go outside today because it is 2 degrees and twice a icy as it was yesterday.

In the last two weeks I sprained my ankle twice so I am taking twice as long to heal.

This day only happens twice in every 200 hundred years.

Maybe I just want an excuse two sit down for a damn minute.

To tell you the truth Twosday has been as magical as the numbers it suggest it may be.
As far as I can see with my two eyes, I see a new future in the century starting with 2000. After all the next day is always the future.

Twomorrow is 2/23/2022 which adds up to 13.

Well that's an entirely different conversation, now isn't it.

DREAM QUEEN.

I Dreamt Up a Film Festival

I founded a film festival

I got it in a dream.

It sounded like a simple thing to do,

After all, I am the dream queen

I dreamt up a café

I dreamt up some songs

I dreamt up a play and books and things

For you could play along…

So the dream came true

and now submissions are due.

Stars came to wave

and audiences came to clap.

Four times latter,

I became a filmmakers waiter.

Happy to help, I put my money and time on the shelf to

Serve other's dreams,

because after all I am the dream queen.

A WOMAN THING

Don't read this if you are a man.
God knows, I love men, but I just have throw out a broad sweeping truth about how we woman think about you men.
Here we go…

We are sick of your bullshit.

We don't care what color you are really. We are still sick of your bullshit.

The same shit happens in every country between men and woman. Men cause wars, rape women, abuse children, control money and run governments that make the rules.

So pretty much, we're sick of your bullshit.

We don't care if your gay or think you are an exception to the rule among men. We are still sick of your bullshit.

It doesn't matter if you have helped lots of women monetarily or gave us jobs. We're are sick of your bullshit.

Hopefully we can help men understand we are sick of their bullshit without having to make ourselves so

damn small and innocently apologetic that they can
still tell…
we are sick of bullshit.

MY MOTHER DIED

It took me a few years to start writing again after I lost my Mother. It's 2022 now. I lost her in 2017.

It feels like she just died. I still pick up the phone to call her. It seems like the only thing I can talk about still. I just be boring as hell to listen to.

Because she was the only woman in my family that I spent every day with as a child, and so had six brothers and a Father, we felt out numbered.

We were out numbered. My Mother's Mother died when she was 10. She had no sisters only three brothers.

She was always out numbered.

But she made up for it. She became everyone's number 1.

The most loved,
The best cook,
The one people came to and counted on and listened to. She was a Queen.

She outnumbered everyone and she could do it dancing backwards.

See you someday again in person Mama. Thanks for your guts. Thanks for your rings and thanks for the hats. You know what I mean.

This book is dedicated to you. You are one remarkable Spirit in the Universe. Peace out Lodi.

Your little girl,

Katie

I GOT A DOG

Her name is Lacey.

She is a child in a puppy costume,

She hates her regular clothes

Who knew that I would become a Mom late in life…
but I did.
I think my Mother sent her. She knew that I always wanted a daughter because my Mother always made me feel that she was so grateful to have a daughter, even though she said I was a pain in the ass to raise sometimes ☺

When I asked her if I was worth it, she told me I made her life worth something it would not have been if not for me.

I understand now. I'm a slow learner.

ATM
↑ RESTRO
ELEVAT
COAT

www.ingramcontent.com/pod-product-compliance
Lightning Source LLC
Chambersburg PA
CBHW071202300726
48975CB00004B/1256